Original title:

A Symphony of Leaves

Copyright © 2025 Creative Arts Management OÜ

All rights reserved.

Author: Natalia Harrington

ISBN HARDBACK: 978-1-80581-834-2

ISBN PAPERBACK: 978-1-80581-361-3

ISBN EBOOK: 978-1-80581-834-2

Windswept Verses

In the park, how they twirl,
Dancing madly, a leafy swirl.
They giggle as they twine,
Chasing squirrels, feeling fine.

A gust comes, off they race,
Playing tag in a leafy chase.
They tumble, flip, and glide,
In this green parade, they slide.

Whispers of jokes on the breeze,
Tickling trunks and teasing trees.
They flutter, poke, and tease,
Making fun of every sneeze.

But watch out! A strong wind's near,
"Hurry up!" they laugh and cheer.
They scramble, sway, and jive,
In this leafy world, they thrive!

On Autumn's Breath

The trees are wearing colors bright,
In their dance, they share delight.
Leaves falling down like popcorn swift,
Nature's joke, a playful gift.

Wind talks secrets to the ground,
While squirrels plot without a sound.
Chasing leaves in dizzy trails,
Their acorns roll like tiny sails.

Songs of the Shifting Atmosphere

The breeze hums tunes of laughter loud,
While leaves form bands to gather a crowd.
They flap their arms like jazzing fools,
Swinging low in nature's schools.

In choreography, they twist and twirl,
A leaf ballet in a leafy whirl.
Each gust a cue—and off they fly,
To tickle noses, oh my oh my!

Revelations in the Understory

In shadows where the whispers creep,
Mice trade jokes with a giggling heap.
Leaves eavesdrop on the fun below,
Cracking wise as winds gently blow.

A rabbit hops, a fox takes note,
While fungi take their mushroom vote.
Amidst the chatter, secrets unfold,
Nature's stand-up act—a joy to behold!

The Poetry of Earth's Palette

With every hue, the earth's a muse,
Painting laughs in reds and blues.
Leaves share punchlines that tickle the air,
In the gallery, no need to be fair.

A brush of red, a dash of gold,
Stories in colors, funny and bold.
While nature giggles in festive glee,
Every season laughs—just wait and see!

Echoes of Wind and Wood

The trees wear hats of yellow and red,
As squirrels plan parties in their cozy bed.
Branches wave like they're leading a band,
While acorns drop down, just like they planned!

A gust of breeze plays peek-a-boo,
Leaves twist and twirl, just like a crew.
Nature's jesters laugh in the sun,
Making us giggle, oh what fun!

Harmonious Embrace of Color

The maples gossip with the oaks so tall,
Trading secrets as the leaves start to fall.
A painter's palette spills on the ground,
Those colorful whispers, oh, what a sound!

Frolicking leaves in shades of delight,
Ballet in the breeze, what a sight!
Dancing on lawns, they shuffle and glide,
Pretending they're boats on a fun leaf tide.

Conversations in the Autumn Mist

The fog rolls in like a shy little friend,
Leaves giggle softly, whatever they send.
Branches reach out, sharing tall tales,
As critters make plans for their fanciful trails.

Mice in their scarves squeak songs of the day,
While chipmunks keep drama in their own play.
Whispers of nature fill the cool air,
Those secrets of autumn, beyond compare!

Whispers of Vermilion and Gold

Golden leaves blush as the sun's shifting light,
Tickling the branches, oh, what a sight!
Chirpy birds chuckle at the flying leaves,
While deer strut about, pinching their sleeves.

In a grand promenade, they prance and they sway,
Announcing the arrival of leaf-ballet day.
Nature's own jesters, with flair and with glee,
All join together for a fun jamboree!

Celestial Patterns Above

Breezes dance like cheeky sprites,
Leaves play games in sunny heights.
They twirl and spin, oh what a sight!
Nature's jesters, pure delight.

Squirrels eye them with great glee,
Plotting acorns, wild and free.
But leaves just laugh and glide away,
In this leafy, woozy play.

Vibrant Cascades of Color

Crimson dares the orange hue,
Yellow giggles, what a view!
They tumble down, a wild parade,
While grasses cheer, in sunlit shade.

The wind's a prankster, pulling pranks,
Leaves tumble down like silly swanks.
In every swirl, a chuckle found,
Nature's jesters all around.

Nature's Harmonious Canvas

Whispers rustle in the trees,
Giggles float upon the breeze.
Each leaf holds a silly song,
As creatures join in all along.

The branches sway with glee, no doubt,
While squirrels chatter, dance about.
Colors clash in joyful cheer,
A canvas bright, the reason's clear.

A Tantalizing Tangle

A twist, a turn, oh look at that!
Leaves engaging in a spat.
They tangle close, like best of friends,
Creating trouble that never ends.

A flutter here, a wobble there,
Barking dogs with leaves to share.
With every giggle, they might fall,
A leafy thrill, a nature brawl.

The Rustle of Dreams

In a garden where whispers play,
The leaves wiggle, have their say.
Squirrels dance with acorn hats,
While grasshoppers wear polka-dots.

Breezes tickle, see them flee,
Chasing shadows, oh so free.
Roots gossip 'neath the ground,
With secrets waiting to be found.

Nature's Soft Tones

The branches chuckle, what a clown,
While petals twirl, never frown.
Bees get busy, buzzing loud,
Telling tales to every crowd.

The wind whispers in punning breeze,
As ripples tease among the trees.
Each twig a jester, in the sun,
Nature's comedy has just begun.

Lush Melodies in the Breeze

The sun beats down with a wink and nod,
As flowers sway, they applaud and prod.
The daisies gossip, the roses roll,
In this green space, they find their soul.

A puddle's laugh, a raindrop's song,
Every twig joins in the throng.
With every gust, a giggle flies,
In verdant realms, with silly sighs.

A Tapestry of Green and Gold

In a canvas of colors, wild and bright,
Leaves gather round to share their plight.
A dandelion dons its crown of fluff,
While elder trees scoff, 'Aren't we tough?'

The sun dips low with a rogueish grin,
While shadows pretend they can't begin.
Oh, what folly in the twilight's grace,
Each leaf a player in this merry race!

Serenade of the Changing Seasons

In spring, the blooms throw a dance,
As bees buzz by in a joyful trance.
Summer's heat brings a panting sigh,
While squirrels giggle and squirrels fly.

Autumn's leaves fall with a floppy twirl,
The pumpkins grin, and the scarecrows whirl.
Winter comes with a fluffy kiss,
Snowmen chuckle, oh what a bliss!

The Fibonacci Treetops

Branches spiral high with glee,
A math riddle hanging from a tree.
Numbers leap in the breezy air,
Squirrels whisper, 'Do you dare?'

Round and round the trunks they twine,
Counting acorns like 'one, two, nine!'
Leaves swirl down in a wacky dance,
Nature's numbers put us in a trance.

Cacophony of Colors

Red, orange, yellow, they shout out loud,
Each leaf a member of a crazy crowd.
They tickle each other in the cool breeze,
As pumpkins play tag with the rustling leaves.

Brown leaves grumble, 'We're old and wise!'
While green sprouts giggle, 'We're just a surprise!'
Colors collide in a cheerful brew,
Nature's palette, a silly zoo!

Leafy Echoes of Dusk

At dusk, the leaves start their chatter,
'Did you see that?' Oh, the pitter-patter!
They shade the ground like a giggling dream,
Winking at stars with a leafy beam.

The wind joins in with a rustling laugh,
Tickling branches on its windy path.
Moonlight dances on their glossy sheen,
'Who's the fairest?' they preen and preen!

Echoes of Golden Hues

A squirrel danced in bright sunlight,
Chasing shadows with all its might.
It leapt and twirled, what a sight!
While leaves giggled, taking flight.

A rustle here, a flutter there,
Whispers traveling through the air.
"Don't fall yet!" the branches tease,
As acorns roll down with the breeze.

Treetop Harmonies

Bamboo giggles when the wind blows,
While willow bows with graceful prose.
Cedar joins in with a deep laugh,
As firs tell tales of the past half.

A chorus of rustles, a quirky beat,
Where chirping crickets take a seat.
A symphony of nature, oh so strange,
As trees swap jokes and rearrange.

The Leafy Overture

Maples twirl in a dizzy dance,
While oaks don hats—they take a chance.
Pines crack jokes, with a needle's grin,
As saplings laugh and shout, "Let's begin!"

The sun peeks in to hear the song,
While summer bugs hum along.
But just when they hit the high note,
A gust of wind sends them off-boat!

Lullabies Beneath the Bark

Under the shade, the critters play,
Chasing the boredom of the day.
A turtle sings, oh so slow,
While crickets join in to steal the show.

Branches sway like a lullaby,
Caterpillars munch, oh my, oh my!
A chorus of giggles, a rustling spree,
As nature winks, just wait and see!

Swaying Rituals at Dusk

In the twilight glow they dance,
Leaves in gowns, take a chance.
Wind whispers jokes in their ears,
Tickling trunks with silly fears.

Branches sway with a groan,
"Hey, don't leave me here alone!"
Laughter rustles through the trees,
As squirrels giggle in the breeze.

The shadows play tag all night,
While crickets cheer with delight.
Bouncing off an old oak's side,
Leaves giggle while the boughs glide.

As the stars blink out their eyes,
Twinkling with mischief and sighs.
The leaves plot a prank so sly,
Under the moon's watchful eye.

Ballad of the Wandering Leaves

Once a leaf with dreams so grand,
Decided to leave its homeland.
It swayed off on an autumn quest,
In search of fun, it thought was best.

It danced with winds, a cheeky sprite,
And found a friend, a squirrel bright.
Together they rolled down the hill,
Cracking jokes, their laughter's thrill.

On a journey through colors loud,
They spun 'round in a giggling cloud.
But soon they found that they were lost,
The map was blown, oh what a cost!

They laughed it off, a grand charade,
In leafy costumes, mischief played.
Through every twist, a laughter weaves,
In tales of wandering, oh how leaves tease!

Resounding through the Boughs

A rustling chorus fills the air,
As leaves relate their tales with flair.
Falling down to make a scene,
Like actors, silly and obscene.

"Hey, watch my flip!" one leaf would shout,
It somersaulted, bold and stout.
While others quipped, "You call that grace?"
And burst out laughing, just in case.

The old oak chuckled, wise and stout,
"Remember well what fun's about!"
Leaves flapped their arms, a chuckling crowd,
As the forest echoed, warm and proud.

Morning light brought a new refrain,
Yet still they joke and sing again.
In the woods where laughter thrives,
A circus of whimsy surely survives.

The Story of Seasons Told

Once a leaf began to weave,
A story that none would believe.
It fluttered forth like a wise old sage,
"A tale of seasons, turn the page."

Spring giggled with a floral grace,
While summer came, a warm embrace.
Autumn tossed in colors bright,
And winter brought snow, pure and white.

"They say I'm just a flake," said one,
As snowflakes danced, having fun.
"I'll drift away on a chilly breeze,"
Then sparkled down with playful ease.

Leaves laughed loud, from tree to tree,
Sharing joy, so wild and free.
In every twist of the year's embrace,
Laughter echoes, leaves leave a trace.

Rustling Revelations

In the park, the trees conspire,
Their whispers rise and never tire.
A squirrel with acorns on his head,
Claims he's royal, than all he fled.

Leaves giggle, as they tumble down,
Joining forces to prank the town.
A dance on the breeze, oh so bright,
They twirl 'round the dog with delight!

The pigeons roll their eyes and stare,
At the chaos that fills the air.
One leaf lands right on a man's hat,
He grins, confused — what's this, a cat?

As twilight falls, they sit and sway,
Chortling softly, they've had their play.
"Come back tomorrow!" the branches cheer,
"We'll keep defying gravity here!"

Fragments of a Breezy Sonnet

In the wind, a leaf does prance,
To a tune of nature's dance.
A breeze can't help but join the fray,
Tickling noses in a merry way.

Dandelion puffs take to the sky,
Like tiny ships, oh me, oh my!
They sail past birds with quizzical looks,
Trading gossip with all the crooks.

Branches bob, they know the score,
While acorns plop - oh, what a bore!
But wait! A nut has found a muse,
And here we go, it's a leafy ruse!

As night descends, with twinkle clear,
The leaves declare, "We'll dance all year!"
To the rhythm of the stars above,
They laugh and twirl, in leafy love.

Herald of the Harvest

In the orchard, fruits do play,
With leaves that tickle in a fray.
An apple shouts, "I'm going to fall!"
While laughing pears say, "Not at all!"

The pumpkins grin, all orange and round,
Wishing they could leap off the ground.
"If we roll, we'll cause a scene!"
They chuckle at the cornfield green.

The scarecrow struts, a splendid sight,
With leaves that dance in pure delight.
He waves his arms, the fruits all quake,
In a giggly game that they all make.

As twilight glows, they share old tales,
Of windy days and feathered trails.
A harvest moon gives a wink and nod,
While they chuckle, thanking the god!

The Bark's Silent Echo

In the woods, there's a trunk with style,
Who watches all with a wooden smile.
"Tell me a joke," the birch does plead,
As leaves tumble down, taking heed.

A pine concedes, "I've got a few,
But watch your step - they stick like glue!"
Chuckles ripple through the green expanse,
As a dewdrop slips and starts to dance.

The bark cracks wise, "What's wood without knots?
Just asking, but I've got my thoughts!"
Laughter echoes through ages long,
As the forest hums its playful song.

At dusk, they sip the moonlit brew,
Sharing secrets from me to you.
In this charming grove, the fun won't cease,
For here, with leaves, all worries release!

Canvas of Nature's Palette

Leaves in colors quite absurd,
Painting trees, their daily word.
Yellow giggles, red ones prance,
In the breeze, they love to dance.

Squirrels wear hats made of bark,
While chipmunks sing and leave a mark.
Sunlight dapples with a wink,
Nature's pranks make us rethink.

Acorns tumble down like rain,
Chasing mice, they cause delay.
Each rustle is a sneaky tease,
Nature's laughter in the trees.

Frolicsome winds toss them about,
Leaves play tag, there's no doubt.
An autumn jeu de vivre so bright,
A kaleidoscope of pure delight.

The Wind's Gentle Caress

Whispers from the swirling air,
Leaves giggle without a care.
Tickles from a breezy plume,
Tick-tock, watch the branches bloom!

A crow with style, a hat so neat,
Dances backwards on his feet.
He calls out to the passing breeze,
Join me, friend, let's play with ease!

The gusts wear capes, quite a sight,
Playing tag from morn till night.
In every rustle, there's a song,
Nature's jester all along.

Leaves spin tales they wish to share,
Of acorn dramas, oh so rare.
With laughter hanging in the air,
Even trees can join the flair.

Fluttering Epiphanies

Whirling thoughts on leafy wings,
Nature's whispers, oh what flings!
Each flap and flutter holds a glee,
What could trees wish to decree?

A squirrel plots a nutty scheme,
While leaves giggle, lost in dream.
In the ballet of the boughs,
Who will win? It's up for vows!

The leaves pretend to lose their way,
Chasing birds in a leafy fray.
Seasons toast with farcical cheer,
What's next, I'll leave that unclear!

If they could speak, oh what a jest!
Each tumble down an Eden quest.
Living life in joyful spins,
With every whirl, the laughter begins.

Choreography of Branches

Branches twist in party hats,
Leaves perform like fancy cats.
Jiving in the autumn sun,
Oh, this dance has just begun!

A flip, a flap, a cartwheel bright,
Branches twirl with pure delight.
Bark-encrusted jokers cheer,
What a show, let's bring the beer!

Underneath the leafy sway,
Nature's band starts to play.
Drumming acorns on the ground,
A raucous giggle all around.

Step by step, they form a line,
Chasing wind, oh how divine!
Colors swirling, laughter free,
Join this wild jubilee!

Drenched in Golden Glory

In a park not far from here,
The leaves dance like a cheer,
Wearing coats of gold and red,
Falling fast, avoiding dread.

Squirrels plot a daring heist,
Gathering nuts, oh so nice,
But a leaf slips to the ground,
Landing with a funny sound.

The breeze carries whispers of fun,
As laughter mingles, they outrun,
A game of hide and seek unfolds,
With each twist, a new story told.

So let's prance through this leaf parade,
With every crunch, let's not be afraid,
For in nature's art, we find our glee,
Drenched in laughter, just you and me.

The Ballad Beneath Our Feet

A rustle here, a crunchy beat,
Nature's song beneath our feet,
In colors bright, they shimmy down,
Spinning tales, they wear a crown.

Fallen friends with jokes to share,
A tumble here, a scandal there,
They scare the pigeons as they land,
Playing tricks as nature planned.

Laughter echoes with each square foot,
Silly dances as we scoot,
Who knew that such a scene could be,
A giggle fest of hilarity?

So stomp around, please don't be shy,
Join the leaves as they sigh, fly high,
A dance of joy, a mischievous feat,
In the ballad beneath our feet.

Waltz Amongst the Maple's Dance

Maples twirl, red skirts afloat,
Whisper secrets on a goat,
While acorns giggle, rolling 'round,
Making mischief on the ground.

With each gust, a chuckle spreads,
As leaves tease the sleepy meds,
Crafting shadows, just for fun,
In a leaf waltz, 'til day is done.

Side by side, they prance and sway,
Making fun of the sunny day,
A leaf slips, the laughter grows,
Nature's slapstick in prose.

So let's twirl in this glorious mess,
With a wink, let's not digress,
For in this dance, so swift and bright,
Lies comedy in leaf-filled sight.

The Paintings of Autumn Skies

The trees wear costumes of pure gold,
As stories of autumn, brightly told,
A canvas of humor, the sky so wide,
Leaves laugh, swaying side by side.

A paintbrush dipped in a pumpkin hue,
As critters sashay, just for you,
With vibrant strokes, they smear the ground,
In this gallery, laughter's found.

Squirrels sketch as acorns roll,
Critiquing leaves, that's their goal,
Witty remarks fly like a kite,
In these paintings, joy's the light.

Join the charm in this playful spree,
Where every leaf invites you and me,
For autumn's brush with colors bold,
We are the stories that unfold.

The Sigh of Autumn Winds

Whispers float through tree-lined streets,
Squirrels plot their sneaky feats.
Leaves giggle, dancing in the air,
"Catch us if you can!" they declare.

Crisp and crunchy, they swirl around,
Tickling shoes upon the ground.
Piles grow high, a leafy mound,
Of treasure waiting to be found.

Every gust, a playful tease,
Branches sway with charming ease.
The wind, a mischievous friend,
Creating chaos that won't end.

So join the fun, don't just stand still,
Leap in a pile — it's a thrill!
Laughing leaves in joyful sound,
The autumn breeze knows no bound.

Cascading Verses from Above

From heights above, the boughs spill ink,
In autumn's art, we stop and think.
A splash of gold, a dash of red,
Nature's scribbles overhead.

Each leaf's a note, a giggle, a cheer,
They waltz and swirl, then laugh in shear.
Falling down, they play pretend,
Hiding 'til the chilly end.

With every rustle, a joke is told,
Trees hold secrets, both shy and bold.
"I'm a star!" one leaf proclaims,
As it pirouettes in golden flames.

A party starts when winds arrive,
Leaves in capers, oh how they thrive!
Gather 'round, be part of the scene,
Where every swirl feels like a dream.

Leafy Whirlwinds

Twirl and whirl, a leafy spree,
Nature's dancers, wild and free.
They spin and laugh, a sight to see,
A whirlpool of colors, jubilee!

"Catch me if you can!" one leaf shouts,
As it flutters round in playful bouts.
An acorn plops with quite the clout,
Creating giggles, there's no doubt!

They swirl in circles, leaping high,
Daring squirrels to give it a try.
With laughter heard from every side,
In every gust, the joy can't hide.

So join the leaf dance, shake a limb,
Where fall's the time, the world's in trim.
Nature's jesters on a spinning spree,
Each day a joke, so wild and free!

Nature's Secret Choir

High above, they chatter and sing,
Leaves in harmony, what joy they bring!
Their whispers blend, a comedic choir,
Tickling tree trunks, never tire.

"Save me a seat!" one leaf pokes fun,
"I'm the star of this show, run, run!"
Branches nod, "Oh, what a treat,
To hear you all and feel the beat!"

Rustling notes weave a playful tune,
A round of giggles 'neath the harvest moon.
Every breeze, a conductor's hand,
Leaves applaud as they start to stand.

So spill your laughter, don't hold it back,
Join the chorus; never lack!
In nature's choir, so light, so bright,
Bring on the laughter, ignite the night!

Twirling with the Wind's Embrace

Leaves dance around, a silly swirl,
Caught in a breeze, they twirl and twirl.
One takes a dive, then makes a blunder,
Lands on a dog, now that's a wonder!

Chasing each other, like kids at play,
Whispering secrets, come what may.
Laughter erupts as they flop and sway,
Nature's jesters, brightening the day.

Caught in a gust, they stumble and flip,
A pirouette here, then off on a trip.
Giggling gales, what a hoot to see,
Leaves cracking jokes, carefree and free!

They huddle together, a clumsy parade,
Slipping and sliding, a grand charade.
With each rustling cackle, they set the scene,
In this leafy ballet, they reign supreme!

Brushstrokes of Life and Loss

A crisp orange leaf in the autumn glare,
Dreams of a branch, now kissed with air.
Once so vibrant, a vibrant cheer,
Now makes a pillow for a sleeping deer.

Each fallen friend, a memory quick,
Leaves in the wind, they play hide and seek.
One chatters loudly, while others just sing,
A racket of colors that the season brings.

Crimson, yellow, all jumbled in jest,
Fighting for space in nature's grand quest.
A brushstroke of laughter, a splash of surprise,
In this fleeting canvas, what joy lies!

Oh, the tales they tell on the ground below,
Of all the adventures they've come to know.
A gallery bursting with giggles and grins,
In brushstrokes of chaos, where humor begins.

Tones of the Verdant Stage

On the verdant stage, the leaves take a bow,
With a clap and a cheer, they steal the show now.
Twisting and turning, with flair and a wink,
They crack up the crowd; oh, what do you think?

A chorus of greens sing their funny refrain,
Tickling the air, light as a plane.
Maroon, olive, and gold in the mix,
Delivering punch lines with whimsical tricks.

In the spotlight's glow, they leap and they dive,
Keeping the spirit of fun alive.
With each rustling note, they tumble and sway,
On this verdant stage, it's a leaf cabaret!

A ricochet here, and a flounce over there,
Leaves take to laughter, without any care.
Finding their rhythm, they cha-cha with glee,
A concert of colors, anarchy set free!

The Swaying Ballet of Spheres

In circles they spin, those orbs of green,
A whimsical ballet, quite the scene.
Round and round, they whirl with delight,
Tumbling in laughter, it's quite a sight.

A twist from the oak, a jump from the pine,
Each leaf joins the dance, feeling so fine.
Giggling branches, how they glide and sway,
A parade of spheres, come laugh and play.

Every pirouette, a chuckle they share,
Joyful uproar, filling the air.
With twinkling eyes, they daintily prance,
In this leaf ballet, they find their chance.

Floating around, they tickle the trees,
Playful companions, carried with ease.
At the end of the show, the applause is sincere,
For in this gentle waltz, joy is always near!

Autumn's Gentle Serenade

In the breeze, they twirl and dance,
Wearing colors like a bold romance.
They tumble down with such delight,
Whispering jokes in the fading light.

A leaf slips past a cheeky squirrel,
Who stumbles back, does a little whirl.
Raking piles become a slide,
Where giggles of critters cannot hide.

Acorns drop with a mighty sound,
As squirrels gather round and bound.
They chatter away like old pals do,
While branches shake with a playful 'boo!'

Each gust of wind brings playful flares,
Leaves chuckle softly without any cares.
In this season, laughter is the key,
Nature's antics for all to see!

The Language of Rustling Foliage

Whispers flutter from trees up high,
As leaves debate the clouds in the sky.
One says, 'I'm green, then I'm brown!',
The others giggle, 'That's a foolish gown!'

A gust comes by and steals their hats,
Leaving behind just tattered spats.
With shouts of glee, they leap and sway,
Their rustling talk is lively play.

Branches sway like they're at a ball,
While acorns bounce, they're having a ball!
A disco party on the forest floor,
With funky moves, they twirl and explore.

Oh, the playful banter in the air,
As leaves show off their carefree flair.
Crisp crunching underfoot ignites,
A symphony of giggles, pure delights!

Melodies of the Forest Floor

Step right up, to the leaf parade,
Where crunching sounds begin to invade.
Every footfall's a rhythmic beat,
As leaves join in for a dancy treat.

Here twigs play tunes like flutes so rare,
While rubies and gold sway everywhere.
Pinecones roll like comical balls,
Announcing their presence with joyful calls.

A chipmunk plays tambourine in glee,
Gathering friends for this wild jamboree.
As a stumpy mushroom takes center stage,
A grand performance fit for a sage!

Fallen leaves, with their tales to tell,
In every crinkle, they ring a bell.
So join the fun on this forest floor,
Where nature's laughter is forever more!

Chorus of the Changing Seasons

Colors splash like paint on a canvas,
Leaves are ready for winter's fabulous.
They whisper secrets, make a sound,
As they dance about, swirling around.

Beneath the trees, a merry crew,
Gathering nuts, a silly zoo!
Rabbits hop and raccoons grin,
As their leafy jokes begin to spin.

The elder tree grumbles wise remarks,
While younger leaves giggle, creating sparks.
'Why fall, when you can fly?' they tease,
As a gust pulls them, without any ease.

But oh, when winter calls its bluff,
The leaves concede, they've had enough.
Yet their laughter lingers in the breeze,
Promising spring with all its ease!

Beneath the Canopy's Embrace

I sat beneath a leafy crown,
Where squirrels wear a frown.
They chattered loud, in perfect sync,
As if they all had time to think.

A bird dropped nuts like silly rain,
And landed straight upon my brain.
With acorns bouncing all around,
Nature's giggles were profound.

The breeze whispered little jokes,
While ants marched past in tiny cloaks.
An epic dance, the foliage swayed,
Like it was in a grand parade.

I laughed so hard I shook the ground,
The trees just shrugged, but never frowned.
In this green realm where laughter thrives,
I found my joy, amidst the lives.

Rhythms of the Wild

Bees buzzed to a funky beat,
While bugs did tap their tiny feet.
A frog croaked loud, conductor's glee,
And crickets played the symphony.

A squirrel in shades lost the plot,
Caught grooving near a steaming pot.
The flowers waltzed in flowered gowns,
As raccoons twirled with silly frowns.

The wind became a wild DJ,
Spin us a tale, we'd dance all day!
As night fell down, the stars blinked bright,
Nature's party, pure delight.

Twirling leaves, and laughing sprites,
In this groove, all wrong feels right.
With every rustle, a jest is made,
In the wild's embrace, we serenade.

Trails of Sticky Amber

Walking paths of gooey gold,
Where sticky tales of trees unfold.
With laughter thick as syrup flows,
While squirrels giggle at their woes.

A conifer's a sticky friend,
Offering hugs that never end.
With sap dripped down upon my shoe,
I join the spree, but not on cue!

Bees buzzing by like tiny cars,
In colliding trails 'neath moonlit stars.
I slip and slide, a clumsy show,
Nature's slapstick, don't you know?

With each new splat, I just can't quit,
Right over rocks, I take a hit.
Sticky amber, what a ride,
In this wild, we all abide!

Conversations in the Shade

Underneath the leafy veil,
I heard the trees begin to wail.
With each complaint of bark and bough,
They quibbled loud, and would not bow.

A raccoon winked and shared a yarn,
About a fruit that caused alarm.
The fruits all giggled, "Not so sweet!"
As plans were made to dance and greet.

In sun-dappled quiet, they conspired,
While ants served snacks, the crowd inspired.
The roots entwined, their tales a throng,
Making histories, all day long.

So here I sit with nature's crew,
While laughter grows and joy breaks through.
In the shade where fun's the norm,
Conversations spark, a playful swarm.

The Quiet Euphony of Nature

In the garden, chirps abound,
A squirrel plays a silent sound.
The flowers giggle at the bee,
Buzzing around like it's carefree.

The bushes rustle with a grin,
A pigeon plops; let games begin!
The sun peeks in with a jest,
Nature's humor is at its best.

A butterfly, with flapping flair,
Teases a cat who's unaware.
They dance and prance, a crazy chase,
While daisies shake their leafy base.

Each sunbeam tickles all around,
And laughter echoes in the ground.
The trees join in, a swaying cheer,
A concert no one else can hear.

Shadowed Melodies

The shadows dance, they twirl and spin,
Underneath the trees, a playful din.
A raccoon tiptoes, wearing a mask,
In search of snacks—it's a noble task!

The wind whispers jokes into the night,
Leaves chuckle softly, what a delight!
A crabapple drops with a thud,
Sending squirrels leaping through the mud.

The moon winks down with a cheeky grin,
While crickets chirp as if to spin.
With foliage swaying to the tune,
Nature's giggle under the moon.

The night serenades with a soft hum,
As shadows laugh, oh what fun!
In this quiet, the world's alive,
With merry sounds that thrive and jive.

Leafy Dialogues at Dawn

As dawn breaks light, leaves start to chat,
A robin listens, perched on a hat.
"Did you see the frog? What a leap!"
"Quite impressive, I'd say—hop not creep!"

The daisies gossip, sharing their dreams,
"Yesterday's rain made us bursting at the seams!"
The daisies snicker at a dandelion,
"Your fluff's quite a sight, just like a lion!"

Squirrels chime in, tails held high,
"Gather the acorns; oh me, oh my!"
While leaves debate what colors to wear,
In this grand meeting, fun fills the air.

As morning stretches, the laughter grows,
Every blade of grass with a quip, it knows.
In leafy dialogues, they toast the dawn,
With cuddly warmth, the day's drawn on.

Embraced by the Emerald

In a world of green where giggles soar,
The tall grass sways, begging for more.
"Tickle me, sunshine!" the leaves seem to cry,
As ants parade, in single file, they fly.

The branches creak in a comical tune,
While bees conduct, buzzing with a swoon.
"Don't forget us!" chirps a nearby crow,
"Without our banter, where would you go?"

A grasshopper hops, with rhythm and flair,
He tells his neighbor, "I'm light as air!"
"Let's race!" shouts a gopher, poking his head,
But someone just giggled; he's still in bed.

As day unfolds, each leaf finds its role,
In this frolicsome dance, nature's soul.
Together they giggle, a raucous cheer,
Embraced by the emerald, joy is near!

Interludes in Nature's Gallery

In the park, the trees did tease,
With whispers and a rustling breeze.
Squirrels danced with acorn hats,
Chasing shadows, springy chats.

A leaf dropped down, took a bow,
Fell right on a lady's brow.
She laughed, then danced, what a sight,
Joining nature in delight.

Birds chattered in a comedy,
Each tweet a quirky melody.
Rabbits hopped, their tails a blur,
Dodging all the falling fur.

As sunset painted a bright scene,
Critters gathered, wild and keen.
Nature's laughter fills the air,
A gallery of joy right there.

Tribute to the Ancients

Old oaks stand with wisdom deep,
While ivy whispers secrets they keep.
Nutty squirrels plot their surprise,
As wise leaves roll their leafy eyes.

The branches hold a jest or two,
Ancient trees sharing their view.
One said, 'I was here before,
You kids have so much to explore!'

Mossy trunks begin to sway,
As if to say, 'Do it our way!'
Slippers on, the toads will leap,
While judgy ferns all secretly peep.

Gnarled roots break into a dance,
While ancient leaves prance in a trance.
All hail the old with laughter loud,
Roots and stems, so very proud.

The Great Canopy's Refrain

High above, the leaves conspire,
To form a tale of wild desire.
Swaying to the breeze's beat,
With every shuffle, what a treat!

A crow caws out a silly line,
As squirrels tumble, feeling fine.
Leaves giggle as the sun shines bright,
Playing tag with shadows, what a sight!

Branches stretch and take a bow,
'You think you're fast? Just watch me now!'
While nuts drop down like nature's confetti,
Creating joy, oh, so ready!

The fluttering leaves bow in jest,
Pointing out the slowest quest.
Among the pines, all join the plot,
In the canopy, laughing a lot!

Revels in the Rooted Realm

Down below, where roots do curl,
Earthworms wiggle in a whirl.
Dancing mushrooms join the funk,
In their caps, a party trunk!

Beetles boast their shiny shells,
While ants play games, ringing bells.
'Come join us!' cries a giddy sprout,
'The fun begins, give a shout!'

A raccoon flips through fallen leaves,
Adventuring like he believes.
'Is that a snack or just a shoe?'
Laughter echoes through the view.

In this realm of earthy glee,
Life's a riddle, wild and free.
With each root, a tale unfolds,
In nature's cradle, laughter holds.

Whispers in the Canopy

Branches giggle, swaying high,
As squirrels plot their pie in the sky.
Wake the birds with a silly song,
While leaves fall down, they won't last long.

In every breeze a cheeky laugh,
Trees gossip about their leafly half.
Breezy chases make dreams collide,
As nature dances, joy can't hide.

Melodies of the Wind

The wind strums jokes on playful strings,
While blossoms twirl with their silly flings.
Ticklish whispers ride the air,
Turning quiet woods into a fair.

A conga line of acorns march,
Missed the memo, but they still arch.
Fluttering tunes make critters prance,
Nature's waltz, join in the dance!

The Dance of Autumn's Palette

Colors clash in a crazy spree,
Red and gold shout, 'Look at me!'
Pumpkins giggle, in fields they roll,
Silly hats for a dog's stroll.

Frolicking foliage, a playful sight,
Leaves confetti in afternoon light.
Watch them tumble, tumble around,
Autumn's parties know no bound!

Rustling Harmonies

Rustling leaves in a talkative throng,
Hand in hand, they'd sing all day long.
Giggles echo in a wooded space,
With every shiver, they share a face.

Dance on the breeze, let's take a stand,
Nature's orchestra in the land.
As branches sway, the laughter grew,
In fun-filled tunes, the world feels new.

The Quiet Requiem of Leaves

In the breeze, the leaves all sigh,
"Are we falling? Oh me, oh my!"
One flutters down with such great flair,
"Catch me, if you can, if you dare!"

A squirrel pauses, munching nuts,
"You think you're graceful? Just look at us!"
He leaps and twirls, a furry tease,
With acorns bouncing off the trees.

The sun peeks in, a playful ray,
"What's this? A dance? I'll join the fray!"
He winks at leaves, they start to sway,
All nature laughing, come what may!

So here we are, a leafy jest,
In nature's laughter, we find rest.
With echoes ringing in the air,
Who knew that leaves could dance with flair?

Echoes of a Forest Soliloquy.

In the quiet woods, a leaf proclaimed,
"I've got the moves, I'm leafly famed!"
With a twirl and spin, it took its stand,
A performance grand, oh so unplanned!

A tree chimed in, "What's all the fuss?"
"Stop showing off! You're just a plus!"
"But watch me shine, like stars above!"
"Too much bravado, where's the love?"

The mushrooms chuckled, all in a row,
"A standing ovation, don't you know?"
The bramble rolled, with laughter loud,
"Join us for giggles, come be proud!"

So amid the boughs, a jest takes flight,
Nature's stage in the glow of light.
A scene like this, none can ignore,
When leaves debate who's best for sure!

Whispers in the Canopy

Leaves whispered secrets, soft and sly,
"I'm the shiniest, oh my, oh my!"
One retorted with a crinkly grin,
"I'm the funniest, let the games begin!"

A branch piped up, "You're just so green,
I'm the oldest, the wisest, seen?"
The wind laughed, swirling all around,
"You leafy folks are quite the crowd!"

The acorns giggled, trying to bounce,
"Can we join in? We want to prounce!"
A rustle echoed, laughter unfurled,
Nature's joy is a wondrous world!

So in the canopy, amidst the fun,
Every leaf dances under the sun.
With whispers of mirth and chuckles light,
Come join the party, day and night!

Dance of the Dappled Sun

The sun peeks in, a dappled sneak,
"Look at me shine! I'm so unique!"
Leaves shimmy in a golden ray,
"We'll show you how we dance and play!"

A chipmunk chuckled, all in a spin,
"The sun's just jealous of all my kin!"
The shadows laughed, twirling with grace,
"In this dance, we've made our place!"

The petals joined in, a colorful cast,
"Together we'll twirl, make moments last!"
A party of joy, in light and cheer,
In this frolicking dance, all draws near!

So as the leaves embrace the fun,
In the warmth of the glowing sun.
Let laughter linger, laughter run,
For in this dance, we've all just won!

Vibrations Beneath the Boughs

In the breeze, the leaves all dance,
They wiggle and jiggle, oh what a chance!
Squirrels join in, with acrobatic flair,
Chasing their tails, without a single care.

A leaf takes a plunge, with a dramatic flair,
"Watch out below!" it calls in despair.
The grass giggles softly, a ticklish delight,
As nature's own party springs to the night.

Oh what a show, under brightening skies,
A curtain of colors with leaves that surprise.
They whisper and chuckle, gales in between,
As branches all sway, like a scene from a dream.

The dance of the bark, with rhythm and rhyme,
Brings us to laughter, in no given time.
Nature's own comedy, a vibrant display,
Leaves laughing together, come join in the play!

Rhythms in the Swaying Branches

Beneath the green canopy, giggles abound,
As leaves sway and twirl, without making a sound
Branches shake hands in a leafy parade,
While acorns drop down like confetti cascade.

A duck strolls by, with a strut so absurd,
Waving to branches, as if they'd heard.
The trees share a joke, it's a real knee-slapper,
Leaves rolling their edges, the laughter gets crappe

Wind whips through, with a mischievous grin,
Spinning the foliage, a waltz to begin.
The bushes all giggle, the flowers join in,
Nature's own laughter, an innocent sin.

As dusk gently settles, they jabber and tease,
Leaves whisper slyly on the light afternoon breeze
They resemble a bunch of jovial friends,
Beneath their bright outfits, the fun never ends!

Harmonic Decay of Foliage

The leaves are all crooning, a funny little tune,
As they fall to the ground, like confetti in June.
A chorus of colors, all swirling around,
The ground's a stage now; oh what a sound!

"Catch me if you can!" the goldsworth declared,
As it floated on down, like it really cared.
The red ones just giggled, all twirling with pride,
While the brown ones looked grumpy, they wanted to hide.

"The branches hum softly, in a rich deep bass,
While twigs join the rhyme in their quirky embrace.
The trees roll their eyes, watching the freefall,
These leaves need a lesson in how to stand tall!"

But despite the decay, it's a rip-roaring sight,
As each leaf cascades, in the warm autumn light.
They remind us that laughter is key to this game,
For when leaves are falling, it's never the same!

The Crescendo of Falling Leaves

The leaves form a line, for a grand leafy show,
They tumble and prance, doing pirouettes low.
A flamboyant display, with no room for fear,
As laughter erupts with each leaf that draws near

A little oak giggles, all yellow and bright,
"Look at that maple, he's taking off flight!"
While pine needles chuckle, all prickly and wise,
Whispering secrets, with a twinkle in their eyes.

With a whoosh and a swirl, they paint the ground go
Twirling in chaos, but never too bold.
The trees shed their layers, a glorious blast,
Creating a stage where memories are cast.

As night settles down, with a flick and a flap,
Leaves write their stories, in a heartfelt clap.
The symphony lingers, as the stars rise above,
A melody crafted, in the season we love!

Choreography of the Forest Floor

In the woods, the critters dance,
Squirrels twirl, not missing a chance.
They leap and spin, such a sight,
Even mushrooms giggle in delight.

The hedgehogs wear tiny shoes,
Practicing their waltz and blues.
Rabbits hop in style, oh what flair,
While old owls clap without a care.

Frogs croak out the bass so deep,
As fireflies flash and never sleep.
The trees sway with a leafy cheer,
Their whispers echo, "We're all here!"

A raccoon conducts with a twig,
Tapping rhythms, oh so big.
Leaves rustle in a playful groove,
Nature's laughter, everybody move!

Nature's Silent Orchestra

Without a sound, the woodland hums,
As squirrels play, the laughter comes.
Beneath the canopy, secrets unfold,
Even the deer tap toes, oh so bold.

Caterpillars play in a line,
Chasing each other, feeling fine.
They wiggle and jiggle under the sun,
Giggles erupt; oh, isn't it fun?

The wind whistles a cheeky tune,
As the flowers sway, it's a colorful boon.
Bees buzz in harmony, round and round,
Creating melodies, rarely sound.

In this quiet show, the creatures greet,
As branches clack, a joyful beat.
Nature's humor, all in delight,
A hidden concert under starlight.

Tones of Twilight Foliage

As daylight fades, colors collide,
The trees giggle, branches wide.
Bamboo shoots sway like they're in a fight,
Tickling the raccoons who dance at night.

Amidst the dusk, the antics increase,
Fireflies blink, a buzzing piece.
Crickets chirp and puns they relay,
While shadows play hide-and-seek away.

The owls hoot a punny line,
"Whooo's ready for a drink of wine?"
Their feathers ruffle in playful jest,
While tree frogs croak their very best.

As leaves crunch underfoot, they pout,
"Stop stepping on us! We're out and about!"
In this twilight, the laughter prevails,
Nature's joke, told in leafy trails.

Lullaby of the Verdant Grove

In the grove, the leaves sigh low,
As sleepy heads sway to and fro.
The bedtime tales of crickets ring,
While the owls whisper secrets of spring.

Under the moon, a hoot takes flight,
Hedgehogs dream of a berry-filled night.
The stars winkle like mischievous elves,
While trees shake their fronds, they're telling themse

"Sleep tight!" the fireflies softly glow,
Lighting up paths, where dreams can flow.
The breeze tickles, it begins to tease,
"Don't snore too loud, or you'll scare the bees!"

As eyelids close with gently creased,
The forest chuckles; it's quite the feast.
Nature's lullaby sings through the dark,
A funny serenade from the heart.

Colors That Speak to the Soul

In the garden, hues collide,
Greens and yellows take a ride.
A purple flower made me sneeze,
Sparks of laughter in the breeze.

Red leaves dance like they're in a race,
Blue ones giggle, a lively chase.
Each swirl and twirl, a vibrant prank,
Nature's jesters in the bank.

Golden petals wave goodnight,
While crickets groan at their delight.
In this mural of shades so bright,
I laugh at leaves as they take flight.

The Crescendo of Nature's Breath

Rustling leaves, a joyful cheer,
Whispering secrets, very near.
A squirrel trills a tuneful joke,
While branches giggle, what a poke!

Wind sings softly, tickling trees,
With every note, I catch a sneeze.
A laugh escapes, as pollen flares,
Nature's humor hanging in the airs.

In harmony, the twigs do sway,
Composing songs in playful play.
A chorus of caws, and chirps abound,
In this concert, joy is found.

Flute of the Forest Breeze

The breeze arrives with a flute-like sound,
Tickling leaves that giggle around.
A playful rustle whispers hello,
As acorns fall, putting on a show.

Branches sway with exaggerated flair,
Nature's dancers without a care.
A beetle hums, a comedic tune,
While shadows play under the moon.

Frogs croak like they've lost their keys,
Trees chuckle softly, secrets tease.
A leaf takes a bow, and then a slide,
Nature's humor on this wild ride.

Emotions among the Oak

The oak tree wears a scruffy grin,
With leaves that twist and turn within.
It sways and creaks, a jolly clown,
Telling tales of roots in town.

Each branch a limb of silly glee,
Whispering love and laughter free.
A robin joins with a chirpy flight,
While wise old owls nod with delight.

With every wiggle of leafy arms,
It shares its heart, unknowing charms.
Emotions tumble, a leaf parade,
In their laughter, joy cascades.

Notes from the Arbor Shadows

In the park where squirrels prance,
Leaves laugh as they skip and dance.
Whispers tickle the trunks so wide,
While ants form a band, all marching side by side.

A raccoon plays drums on an old tin can,
Trees sway like they're part of a jam plan.
Birds chirp out notes, kind of offbeat,
While crickets tap dance with little feet.

The sun winks down, a playful tease,
As we listen to nature's silly breeze.
Each gust has a joke, a chuckle or two,
Leaves giggle softly, just for me and you.

The Call of the Harvest Breeze

Pumpkins roll like bowling balls,
Laughter bounces off the walls.
Corn stalks wave, 'Come join the game!'
As the breezy whispers call your name.

Apples plop off branches above,
Trying to land with a gentle shove.
But sometimes they just do a flop,
And the crows all caw, 'Let's not stop!'

The wind plays tricks, hides behind trees,
Making leaves shimmy like they aim to tease.
Every gust giggles, squeals out loud,
Drawing in everyone, it's quite the crowd!

Soprano Sojourn in the Woods

In the woods, where shadows blend,
Squirrels stretch, not ready to bend.
They hold a concert, tails in a twirl,
While leaves sing high, giving a whirl.

Mice tap dance on mushrooms so bold,
Singing secrets that never get old.
Breezes swirl in a jazzy bout,
While frogs croak solos, no hint of doubt.

A worm takes the stage, with a hat like a king,
Saying, 'Wiggle and evolve, it's the best thing!'
Laughter erupts from the owl in surprise,
As the notes fly up like pies in the skies!

Cadence of the Golden Canopy

Underneath the golden hue,
Leaves debate who'll win, who'll stew.
Rabbits hop to the beat all night,
While the moon chuckles, feeling quite light.

Grass blades sway, whispering cheer,
As we twirl without any fear.
Each step feels like a soft ballet,
With crunching soundtracks, hip-hip-hooray!

A bear rolls by, clapping his paws,
Painting the woods with all the applause.
Nature's giggles echo around,
As we dance on soil, where joy is found!

Tree Top Reveries

In a tree full of chatter, they plot their next play,
With acorn hats and a twig for a bray.
Squirrels chase shadows, bold and spry,
While birds laugh along as they flutter by.

A raccoon in pajamas steals pies from the hive,
Under the moon, it's a wild, crazy jive.
The owls hoot jokes, wise but a bit unclear,
As leaves rustle softly, 'Please, don't interfere!'

The wind plays the flute, and they all take a chance,
As chipmunks join in for a jolly old dance.
With each gentle gust, the branches do sway,
Inviting mischief to frolic and play.

A symphony of giggles fills the night air,
Where whispers of nature tread lightly with care.
As laughter cascades through the boughs overhead,
The trees cozy up, as dreamers are fed.

Wandering with the Currents

Through dappled shadows, the river flows,
With fish in tuxedos, they steal the show.
Frogs leap with flair, croaking rhymes bold,
While turtles in sun hats have tales to be told.

The current giggles, it swirls with delight,
As dragonflies twirl, putting on quite a flight.
A catfish with glasses says, 'I'm quite the catch!'
While a lily pad home is the place to hatch.

Otters are sliding with joy from the banks,
Waving their paws as they do their pranks.
A beaver with dreams of building a spire,
Sinks his own plans without a retire.

So come take a dip in this whimsical stream,
Where laughter and splashes unite in a dream.
In the dance of the currents, all creatures play fair
While bubbles of joy float high in the air.

Nature's Nocturne in Green

Under the moonlight, the crickets confer,
Debating who sings with the best little purr.
A hedgehog recounts his hair-raising tales,
While fireflies twinkle like galloping snails.

The raccoons come out, with masks on their face,
Planning a heist at a picnic's old place.
With cupcakes and cookies, their mission is clear,
Leave no crumb behind, we'll create quite a cheer!'

The owls are wise, but they can't hold a tune,
they hoot out of rhythm beneath the bright moon.
Beneath leafy blankets, the shadows all blend,
A whimsical night, where fun has no end.

In this green theater, all creatures unite,
In laughter and warmth, how they twirl in the night.
A show under stars, in a world so serene,
Nature chuckles softly, 'This is our routine!'

Palette of the Wind's Breath

The leaves take a bow, in hues of delight,
As the wind tickles trees, swirling colors in flight.
A painter with laughter (that's what they say),
Comes to splash joy in the funniest way.

The oranges wiggle, while the reds do a jig,
As yellows twist softly, making each leaf big.
A gust whispers secrets to branches so high,
While whispers turn to giggles, a playful goodbye

With a flick of a stem, and a rustle, a cheer,
The trees all erupt, singing 'Fall is here!'
Dancing to rhythms, each branch knows its role,
In this colorful breeze, they all play their soul.

So join in the fun where the winds have their say,
As laughter and leaves take us far, far away.
In the chase of the zephyrs, the trees all will sway
In a world painted bright, where colors play!

www.ingramcontent.com/pod-product-compliance
Lightning Source LLC
Chambersburg PA
CBHW070308120526
44590CB00017B/2589